RADICAL ACCEPTANCE THERAPY

Your Complete Guide To Inner Reawakening And Self Love Without Fear, Doubt or Shame or Judgement.

Carol Chime

Table of Contents

How To Use This Book..3
PREFACE...10
CHAPTER I: The Path to Radical Acceptance......... 16
CHAPTER II: Awakening to Our True Selves........... 23
CHAPTER III: Healing Relationships...................... 34
CHAPTER IV: Living Fully....................................42
CHAPTER V: Practical Applications...................... 52
Goodbyes.. 59
Glossary of Terms... 67

How To Use This Book

Welcome to "Radical Acceptance Therapy: Your Complete Guide to Inner Reawakening and Self Love Without Fear, Doubt or Shame or Judgment." This book is designed to be your companion on a transformative journey towards greater self-awareness, acceptance, and inner peace. Whether you are new to the concepts of radical acceptance and mindfulness or looking to deepen your existing practice, this guide will provide you with practical tools, insights, and exercises to support your growth.

1. Begin with an Open Mind

Approach this book with curiosity and openness. Radical acceptance is a profound shift in how we relate to ourselves and our experiences, and it may challenge some of your existing beliefs and habits. Allow yourself to explore these concepts without judgment, and be patient with yourself as you integrate new practices into your life.

2. Read Sequentially or Choose Your Path

While the book is structured to build upon each chapter progressively, you can also choose to focus on specific sections that resonate with your current needs. If you are new to these practices, starting from the beginning will provide a comprehensive foundation. If you have specific areas of interest or need immediate guidance, feel free to jump to those sections.

3. Engage with the Practices

Each chapter includes practical exercises and guided meditations designed to help you apply the concepts of radical acceptance in your daily life. Engage fully with these practices, as they are the heart of your journey towards inner reawakening and self-love. Set aside time each day or week to practice mindfulness meditation, self-compassion exercises, and other activities suggested throughout the book.

4. Reflect and Journal

Reflection is a crucial component of personal growth. Use a journal to document your thoughts, feelings, and experiences as you work through the book. Writing down your reflections can help solidify your understanding, track your progress, and provide valuable insights into your journey. Consider answering reflection questions posed at the end of chapters or creating your own prompts based on your experiences.

5. Practice Consistency

Consistency is key to reaping the benefits of radical acceptance and mindfulness. Establish a routine that incorporates the practices discussed in this book. Whether it's daily meditation, weekly reflections, or regular self-compassion exercises, maintaining a consistent practice will deepen your understanding and enhance your progress.

6. *Embrace Setbacks as Learning Opportunities*

The journey of radical acceptance is not linear, and you may encounter setbacks or resistance along the way. Embrace these moments as opportunities for growth rather than failures. Reflect on what triggered the setback, and use the tools and insights from this book to navigate through it with compassion and understanding.

7. *Seek Support and Community*

Personal growth is often enriched by the support of others. Share your journey with friends, family, or a community of like-minded individuals. Discussing your experiences and challenges can provide new perspectives, encouragement, and a sense of connection. If needed, seek guidance from a therapist or counselor who can support you in applying the principles of radical acceptance.

8. Revisit and Reinforce

Revisit sections of the book as needed to reinforce your understanding and practice. Radical acceptance is an ongoing journey, and you may find that certain chapters resonate differently at various stages of your life. Use this book as a reference guide to support your continuous growth and development.

9. Apply What You Learn in Daily Life

The true power of radical acceptance lies in its application to daily life. Use the principles and practices from this book in your interactions with others, in your work, and in how you relate to yourself. By integrating these concepts into your everyday experiences, you will cultivate a deeper sense of peace, resilience, and authenticity.

10. Celebrate Your Progress

Acknowledge and celebrate your progress, no matter how small it may seem. Personal growth is a journey, and each step forward is significant. Recognize your efforts and achievements, and appreciate the positive changes you are making in your life.

This book is more than just a collection of ideas; it is a guide to transforming your relationship with yourself and the world around you. By engaging deeply with its contents, practicing regularly, and approaching your journey with compassion and curiosity, you can cultivate a life of inner reawakening and self-love without fear, doubt, shame, or judgment. Welcome to your journey of radical acceptance.

PREFACE

Welcome to the profound journey of radical acceptance—a transformative practice that encourages us to embrace our lives and ourselves with compassion and clarity. Here, we explore what it means to truly accept every aspect of our existence, learning to navigate our experiences and the world around us with grace and understanding. Through insights from psychology and engaging personal anecdotes, we will discover how embracing radical acceptance can lead to deep healing and inner peace.

Radical acceptance is about affirmatively recognizing reality in all its facets—our joys, sorrows, triumphs, and tribulations—without judgement or resistance. This isn't a passive surrender but an active engagement, a conscious choice to accept things as they are. The beauty of this acceptance lies not in preventing life's challenges but in altering our engagement with them. By accepting life's terms with openness, we lessen our suffering and gain the clarity to respond with wisdom.

The journey begins with self-acceptance. It involves coming to terms with every part of who we are—our strengths and our flaws. By acknowledging and embracing our entire selves, we cultivate a profound self-compassion that then extends outward, improving our relationships and fostering a compassionate view toward others. This process not only enhances our capacity for love but also enriches our interactions with the world.

Throughout this book, you will encounter stories that resonate with universal struggles and triumphs, alongside practical exercises that aim to incorporate radical acceptance into your everyday life. Each chapter will guide you through this practice, helping you to weave acceptance more deeply into your daily experiences. Embracing this practice is both a challenge and a promise—the challenge lies in confronting life with honesty and openness, and the promise is the profound peace and freedom that comes from truly accepting yourself and your life.

Radical acceptance is a journey of continuous practice, where each moment presents an opportunity to respond to life's difficulties with presence rather than judgement. It is also a practice of commitment, requiring us to return, time and again, to our intent to fully engage with our lives as they unfold.

As we move forward, I invite you to immerse yourself in the teachings and reflections presented here. Use this book as a companion on your path to living more fully, loving more deeply, and uncovering the peace that lies within you. Now, let us begin this journey together, where we learn to face life with an open heart and a resilient spirit.

As we embark on this path, it is crucial to address two of the most challenging emotions that impede our ability to practise acceptance: fear and shame. These emotions are significant forces in our lives, influencing our actions, shaping our decisions, and colouring our self-perception and interactions.

Fear is a natural response to perceived threats which prepares our bodies to react. However, in modern contexts, these threats are often not physical but psychological—fears of rejection, failure, or the unknown. Such fears can manifest as anxiety or stress, which may paralyse and prevent us from moving forward.

Shame is an emotion that targets our sense of self-worth. It springs from a belief in our own fundamental inadequacy and can be crippling. It makes us feel unworthy of love and acceptance, casting a long shadow over our lives and limiting our potential for growth.

To understand these emotions better, we look back to their origins, often rooted in our earliest interactions during childhood. Our foundational experiences with caregivers and peers set the stage for how we perceive and react to these feelings. The way we were treated in our formative years—whether our vulnerabilities were supported or ridiculed, whether our mistakes were met with empathy or judgement—shapes our emotional landscapes as adults.

This exploration into fear and shame is not just about recognizing their presence in our lives. It is about understanding their roots and learning how to confront and transform these feelings. By doing so, we pave the way for a life characterised by greater self-acceptance, reduced internal conflict, and a more profound ability to engage with the world in a meaningful and authentic way. Let's take this step together, as we learn to navigate and transform these complex emotional experiences into sources of strength and self-understanding.

CHAPTER I: The Path to Radical Acceptance

Understanding Radical Acceptance

What is Radical Acceptance?

Radical acceptance is a term that resonates deeply for those seeking relief from suffering and a more authentic engagement with life. It is the full embrace of the facts of one's life, in the moment, without protest, excuse, or complaint. It implies an agreement to tolerate the hard realities of life, even when they are far from what we wanted or expected.

At its heart, radical acceptance is about saying yes to life, in its entirety. It is about acknowledging reality as it is right now, not as we wish it to be. This does not mean passive resignation or giving up on one's desires and goals. Rather, it's about recognizing what is out of our control, reducing our suffering through acceptance, and focusing our energy on actions that we can influence.

The Power of Acceptance

The transformative power of acceptance is vast. When we stop fighting reality, we conserve energy that can be redirected to more productive, positive efforts. Acceptance frees us from the constant tension of desire and aversion, the push and pull against life's unfolding narrative. It allows us to deal with life's challenges with dignity and poise, providing a clearer perspective on which battles are worth fighting and which are better let go.

By accepting painful emotions as part of life, we open ourselves to a wider range of experiences, learning not only to endure but also to grow from these challenges. This acceptance can lead to a deeper peace and a profound understanding that many of life's struggles are not personal failings but part of the shared human experience.

Facing Fear and Shame

Recognizing Our Inner Demons
Fear and shame are among the most powerful and disruptive emotions that humans experience. They are the spectres that haunt our inner lives, often holding us back from achieving our full potential. Fear arises as a primal alert to potential danger, an evolutionary tool crucial for survival. However, in modern contexts, it often triggers in the face of emotional vulnerabilities rather than physical threats, leading to anxiety and avoidance behaviours.

Shame, intimately linked with our concept of self, can make us feel fundamentally flawed or inadequate. It is often internalised during early developmental stages through interactions that suggest we are unlovable or unworthy based on our actions or inherent characteristics.

The Roots of Fear and Shame

To truly face our fears and shame, we must understand their origins, which often lie in our earliest experiences. Fear may develop from instances where we felt profoundly threatened or helpless, while shame often grows from situations where we were made to feel unworthy or inherently wrong. These emotions are reinforced by societal expectations and cultural norms that dictate certain behaviours, success standards, and roles, which can further entrench feelings of inadequacy and anxiety.

Addressing these roots involves revisiting painful memories and reevaluating the narratives we've constructed around our identities. It's a process of challenging the validity of these narratives and gradually learning to separate our worth from our fears and perceived shortcomings.

Mindfulness and Compassion

The Practice of Mindfulness
Mindfulness is the basic human ability to be fully present, aware of where we are and what we're doing, and not overly reactive or overwhelmed by what's going on around us. It's about observing our thoughts and feelings without judgement. Mindfulness practice involves various forms of meditation, breathing exercises, and awareness techniques that help anchor us in the present moment.

This practice teaches us to observe our experiences with neutrality, a crucial aspect of radical acceptance. By fostering an attentive and open awareness, mindfulness allows us to see the reality of our situations without the filters of intense emotion or preconceived notions.

Cultivating Self-Compassion

Alongside mindfulness, compassion—particularly self-compassion—is vital in the practice of radical acceptance. Self-compassion involves treating ourselves with the same kindness, concern, and support we'd offer a good friend. When faced with instances of failure or noticing something we don't like about ourselves, self-compassion lets us be gentle and understanding with ourselves instead of harshly critical or judgmentally dismissive.

Developing self-compassion means recognizing that suffering, failure, and imperfection are part of the shared human experience. This shift can dramatically change our perspective, allowing us to connect with ourselves and others more deeply and authentically. Together, mindfulness and self-compassion forge a pathway through which radical acceptance can flourish, enabling us to embrace life with all its imperfections and challenges.

Each of these elements—understanding radical acceptance, facing our fears and shame, and practising mindfulness and compassion—lays a foundation for a richer, more resilient life. As we delve deeper into these practices throughout this book, we invite readers to explore how these principles can be actively integrated into daily living, promoting a more fulfilling and peaceful existence.

CHAPTER II: Awakening to Our True Selves

The Armor of Self-Judgment

Breaking Free from Self-Criticism

Self-judgment is a shield we unconsciously wield against the world's perceived judgments, a protective armor that ironically often causes more harm than protection. This shield comprises harsh self-criticism and relentless standards we impose on ourselves, frequently rooted in our fear of failure and rejection. Breaking free from this cycle of self-criticism requires understanding its origins—typically early experiences where external criticism made us feel vulnerable or inadequate.

To dismantle this armor, we begin by acknowledging that self-criticism has been a misguided form of self-care, intended to protect us from the criticism of others.

Recognizing this, we can gently redirect our intentions, choosing compassion over criticism. This shift involves observing our critical inner voice with curiosity rather than acceptance, questioning its truth and helpfulness. By cultivating an awareness of when and why we deploy this self-criticism, we can start to choose responses that are nurturing rather than destructive, reinforcing our self-worth and competence.

The Effects of Self-Judgment

The impact of self-judgment extends beyond internal turmoil. It influences our relationships, our work, and our ability to embrace life fully. When we are mired in self-judgment, we create a barrier between ourselves and our experiences, filtering life through a lens of inadequacy. This not only colors our personal reality with negativity but also hampers our growth and potential. Persistent self-judgment can lead to anxiety, depression, and a host of other emotional challenges.

Conversely, releasing ourselves from the grips of self-judgment opens up a world of possibilities. It fosters resilience, allowing us to navigate life's ups and downs with greater ease and confidence. Without the constant background noise of self-criticism, we can hear more clearly the voices of our true desires and ambitions. This clarity empowers us to take actions that align more closely with our authentic selves, leading to a more fulfilled and purposeful life.

The Gift of Presence

Being Present with Ourselves

The gift of presence is perhaps the most profound gift we can offer ourselves. Presence means fully engaging with the here and now, embracing each moment with openness and curiosity. Being present with ourselves is not always easy, particularly in today's fast-paced world where distractions abound. Yet, it is essential for true self-awareness and self-acceptance.

To be present with ourselves, we need to cultivate a habit of mindfulness, which allows us to observe our thoughts, feelings, and sensations without judgment. This practice helps us recognize our habitual patterns, including those that lead to self-judgment and self-criticism. Through presence, we can also appreciate the beauty and richness of each moment, whether it's savoring a meal, feeling the warmth of the sun, or simply being aware of our breath.

Techniques for Staying Present

Staying present requires consistent practice. Techniques like focused breathing, mindful walking, and sensory observation can help anchor us in the now. For instance, we can practice deep breathing techniques to center ourselves during stressful moments, or engage in mindful walking to connect with our environment during daily routines. Another effective practice is the 'pause and notice' technique, where several times a day, we pause whatever we're doing to take stock of our current thoughts, feelings, and sensations. This helps build a habit of mindfulness that brings us back to the present.

Embracing Our Vulnerabilities

The Strength in Vulnerability

Vulnerability is often seen as a weakness, but in reality, it is a profound strength. Embracing our vulnerabilities involves acknowledging that we are not perfect, nor do we need to be. It means opening ourselves to the full spectrum of human emotions, including fear, sadness, and uncertainty, and recognizing these feelings as integral parts of our human experience.

The strength in vulnerability lies in its ability to connect us more deeply with others. When we share our true selves, including our fears and flaws, we invite others to do the same, fostering genuine connections built on empathy and understanding. This can lead to richer, more fulfilling relationships and a greater sense of belonging and acceptance.

Sharing Our True Selves

Sharing our true selves is an act of courage. It involves stripping away the facades we often construct to protect ourselves from judgment and rejection. To share our true selves, we must first accept ourselves. This acceptance can be cultivated through practices discussed earlier, such as mindfulness and compassion.

When we share our true selves, we not only liberate ourselves from the constraints of hidden vulnerabilities but also empower others to embrace their own. This sharing can take many forms, from expressing our needs and desires in relationships to presenting our authentic selves in our professional lives. Each act of sharing reinforces our self-acceptance and encourages others to engage with us more openly and authentically.

Through these practices and understandings, "Awakening to Our True Selves" becomes not just a concept but a lived experience. Each step toward embracing our vulnerabilities and sharing our true selves enriches our journey, making us more resilient and more deeply connected to the world around us.

In cultivating these practices, we challenge the conventional narratives around strength and vulnerability, recognizing that true strength comes from authentic self-expression and connection. As we continue to break down the barriers of self-judgment and stay present with our experiences, we discover that our true selves are not static entities, but dynamic aspects of our being that flourish in openness and honesty.

Sharing our true selves also involves a deliberate and often challenging unveiling of who we are at our core—our dreams, fears, passions, and insecurities. This process can feel daunting, as it involves exposing parts of ourselves that we typically shield from the public eye. However, this act of openness not only promotes self-integrity but also invites deeper intimacy and trust in our relationships, creating a supportive network that values authenticity over perfection.

Moreover, as we engage more authentically with ourselves and others, we foster an environment where acceptance is the norm, not the exception. This environment encourages everyone to lower their guards and share their unique perspectives and experiences, enriching the collective human experience. It's a place where people feel safe to be themselves without the fear of judgment, where the diversity of human experiences is celebrated, and where genuine understanding is prioritized over superficial interactions.

In embracing our vulnerabilities, we also learn to manage and mitigate the discomfort that comes with it. Techniques such as self-soothing, seeking support from trusted individuals, and gradually exposing ourselves to our fears can help us navigate this process. By taking small, manageable steps, we build the confidence and resilience needed to face larger challenges. This incremental approach ensures that each experience of vulnerability becomes a building block for greater emotional strength and self-assurance.

Ultimately, the journey of awakening to our true selves is about cultivating a deep sense of self-awareness and self-compassion that guides us through life's challenges and joys. It is about building a life that aligns closely with our values and aspirations, where we are no longer held back by fear or shame but propelled forward by a profound understanding of our own humanity and the shared humanity of others.

This journey requires courage, commitment, and compassion, but the rewards are immeasurable. As we become more attuned to our true selves, we find that life becomes richer and more meaningful. We discover a sense of peace in being authentic, a joy in living according to our true nature, and a profound connection to the world around us that is built on the solid foundation of genuine self-expression.

Thus, as we close this chapter, let us carry forward the lessons of self-acceptance, presence, and vulnerability, integrating them into every aspect of our lives. Let us move boldly into our interactions, cherishing each moment of connection and each opportunity for growth. Let us continue to embrace the beautiful, messy, and wonderfully complex beings that we are, finding strength in our vulnerabilities and peace in our authentic selves.

CHAPTER III: Healing Relationships

Connecting with Others

The Importance of Authentic Relationships

Human beings are inherently social creatures, wired for connection. Authentic relationships, characterized by openness, trust, and deep emotional engagement, are essential to our well-being and happiness. They provide a foundation for mutual growth and support, enhancing our quality of life and our resilience against psychological stress. Authentic relationships require a level of honesty and vulnerability that allows both parties to truly see and be seen without masks or pretenses.

These relationships hold a mirror up to our own selves, reflecting our strengths and weaknesses in ways that solitary reflection cannot. They challenge us to grow, to confront uncomfortable truths, and to stretch beyond our perceived limits. In this light, every interaction has the potential to contribute to our understanding of ourselves and each other, fostering a deeper connection that enriches both individuals.

Overcoming Isolation and Alienation

Despite the interconnected world we live in, many people experience feelings of isolation and alienation. These feelings can stem from a variety of sources, including changing societal structures, personal insecurities, or even past traumas that make trust and openness challenging. Overcoming these feelings is a critical step toward building healthier, more fulfilling relationships.

The first step in overcoming isolation is reaching out. It might start with small gestures of connection, such as engaging in community activities or reaching out to old friends. Each positive interaction builds a bridge, reducing feelings of loneliness and increasing our comfort with closeness. Another crucial aspect is addressing any internal barriers to connection, such as fear of rejection or feelings of unworthiness, often through personal reflection or professional therapy. By tackling these issues, we open ourselves up to the possibility of deeper, more meaningful relationships.

Communicating with Compassion

Mindful Communication

Mindful communication is about being present and fully engaged during interactions with others. It involves listening actively, speaking truthfully, and conveying messages in ways that minimize harm and foster understanding. This form of communication requires self-awareness and self-regulation to manage our emotions and reactions. By focusing on the present moment, we can observe the subtleties of our interactions and adjust our behavior accordingly.

Practicing mindful communication involves several key components: listening with the intent to understand rather than to respond; recognizing our biases and emotions, and how they affect our interactions; and using language that reflects empathy and respect. This approach not only enhances our relationships but also builds a foundation of trust and mutual respect that is essential for resolving conflicts and deepening connections.

Healing Through Dialogue

Dialogue has the power to heal wounds in relationships by addressing misunderstandings and hurt feelings. Effective dialogue involves sharing our own perspectives as well as being open to hearing others' views without judgment. This exchange allows all parties to express their thoughts and emotions in a safe environment, which can lead to breakthroughs in understanding and reconciliation.

Healing dialogue requires patience, courage, and a commitment to resolution. It often involves discussing painful or uncomfortable topics, but by approaching these conversations with compassion and openness, we can initiate the process of healing. Such dialogues help clarify intentions, rectify misconceptions, and strengthen bonds strained by conflict or miscommunication.

Forgiveness and Reconciliation

The Process of Forgiving Others

Forgiveness is a powerful step in the healing process, offering a path out of resentment and anger towards peace and closure. Forgiving others does not mean condoning wrongdoing, nor does it require reconciliation. Instead, it is about letting go of the burden of bitterness and allowing ourselves to move forward.

The process of forgiving others begins with understanding the nature of the hurt and acknowledging its impact on our lives. This often involves empathizing with the person who has wronged us, trying to see the situation from their perspective, and recognizing their humanity. It's a challenging process that requires considerable emotional maturity and strength, but it is also liberating, providing a sense of relief and a clearing of the space that was once filled with negativity.

Self-Forgiveness and Healing

Just as important as forgiving others is forgiving ourselves. Self-forgiveness involves recognizing our own mistakes and accepting that we are fallible and capable of errors just like anyone else. This process is essential for healing and growth, as it prevents self-loathing and chronic guilt from undermining our happiness and self-esteem.

Self-forgiveness requires honesty, patience, and compassion. It often involves reflecting on our actions, understanding the circumstances that led to them, and learning from the experience to avoid future mistakes. By forgiving ourselves, we acknowledge that while we are not perfect, we are worthy of love and happiness—free to move forward with greater wisdom and resilience.

Each of these elements—from connecting authentically with others and communicating with compassion to forgiving and reconciling—plays a crucial role in healing relationships. By integrating these practices into our lives, we foster a healthier, more connected existence, enriched by deep and meaningful relationships that support and sustain us through life's challenges.

CHAPTER IV: Living Fully

Finding Inner Peace

Practices for Inner Calm

Inner peace is a state of calm and contentment that's essential for handling the stress and chaos of everyday life. Achieving this state requires practice and dedication, especially in a world that often values productivity over well-being. Practices for inner calm vary widely, but they all share a common goal: quieting the mind and soothing the spirit.

One effective practice is meditation, which trains the mind to focus and redirect thoughts, promoting a state of relaxation and peace. Techniques such as guided imagery, deep breathing exercises, and progressive muscle relaxation also help reduce stress and enhance emotional well-being. Additionally, establishing a routine that includes regular periods of quiet and solitude can help maintain a calm baseline, allowing you to better manage the inevitable ups and downs of life.

Engaging in regular physical activity, maintaining a nutritious diet, and ensuring adequate sleep are also crucial for mental health and inner peace. Each of these practices contributes to a more balanced and serene mind, making it easier to cope with daily pressures and challenges.

Creating a Peaceful Mind

Creating a peaceful mind goes beyond temporary practices and aims to cultivate a sustained state of tranquility that permeates all aspects of life. This involves not only managing stress but also cultivating attitudes that foster peace, such as acceptance, patience, and compassion.

Mindfulness is particularly effective in creating a peaceful mind. It involves being fully present in the moment, aware of our thoughts, feelings, and surroundings without judgment. This practice helps us become more conscious of our mental habits and reactions that may disrupt our peace, and gradually learn to approach life with a more serene and balanced outlook.

Furthermore, simplifying one's life by reducing commitments, decluttering physical space, and prioritizing meaningful activities can lead to a more peaceful mind. By focusing on what truly matters, you reduce the noise and chaos in your life, paving the way for a deeper sense of peace.

Cultivating Joy and Gratitude

Embracing Joy in Everyday Life

Joy is not merely a spontaneous feeling but a state that can be cultivated and integrated into everyday life, regardless of external circumstances. Embracing joy involves recognizing and appreciating the small pleasures and victories of daily life. This could be as simple as enjoying a quiet cup of coffee in the morning, sharing a laugh with a friend, or appreciating the beauty of nature during a walk.

Activities that spark joy are unique to each individual and require a conscious effort to identify and incorporate them into your routine. Additionally, creating moments of joy can also involve engaging in hobbies or interests that you are passionate about, which not only enriches your life but also adds a sense of fulfillment and satisfaction.

The Practice of Gratitude

Gratitude is a powerful practice that shifts your focus from what is lacking in your life to the abundance that is already present. Keeping a gratitude journal, where you regularly write down things you are thankful for, can significantly increase your awareness of life's blessings and enhance your overall happiness. This practice not only improves mood but also contributes to greater emotional resilience, strengthening your ability to face life's challenges with a positive outlook.

Other methods to cultivate gratitude include expressing thanks to others, reflecting on past experiences that have led to growth, and consciously acknowledging the good in every situation. Over time, these practices train your brain to notice and appreciate the positives, fostering a lasting sense of joy and contentment.

Living with Purpose

Discovering Your Life's Purpose

Living with purpose is about aligning your actions with your core values and passions, creating a meaningful path that not only fulfills you but also contributes to the world. Discovering your life's purpose can be a transformative experience that changes how you view yourself and your role in the world.

This discovery often requires deep introspection and self-reflection. Identifying activities that make you lose track of time, or considering what you would choose to do if money were no object, can provide insights into your passions and potential paths. Additionally, exploring your talents and how they can serve others can help clarify your purpose.

Living a Life of Meaning

Once you identify your purpose, living a life of meaning involves making choices that align with this purpose. This might mean making career changes, adopting new habits, or even altering relationships to support your goals. It requires courage, commitment, and resilience, as aligning your life with your purpose is a dynamic process that evolves along with your experiences and insights.

Living purposefully also enhances your sense of belonging and contribution. It connects you to a larger story, one where your actions make a positive impact on the community and the world. This connection not only enriches your own life but also inspires others to seek their own paths of meaning and fulfillment.

Each of these areas—from finding inner peace and cultivating joy and gratitude to living with purpose—plays a crucial role in achieving a fulfilled and contented life. By integrating these practices into daily living, you open the door to a richer, more vibrant existence, marked by deep satisfaction and a profound sense of accomplishment. This journey is not about reaching a destination of perfection but about continually striving to align more closely with your values and desires, creating a life that resonates with who you are at your core.

Living with purpose also demands a proactive approach to life's challenges. It involves not only celebrating successes but also learning from failures and setbacks. This adaptive mindset ensures that every experience, whether positive or negative, contributes to your growth and helps you refine your path forward.

Moreover, purposeful living impacts those around you by setting a powerful example of intentional living. It can inspire friends, family, and even strangers to reflect on their own lives and consider how they might also live more meaningfully. This ripple effect can extend the benefits of your purpose-driven life far beyond your immediate environment, contributing to a broader cultural shift towards more conscious, considered living.

In summary, the journey to living fully embodied in the practices of finding inner peace, cultivating joy and gratitude, and living with purpose—is a multifaceted and dynamic process. It invites you to explore the deepest parts of yourself, to connect with others in more meaningful ways, and to contribute to the world with your unique talents and insights.

As you move forward, remember that each step on this path enriches not only your own life but also the lives of those around you. The pursuit of inner peace, the cultivation of joy, and the commitment to live purposefully are not just personal goals; they are gifts that you share with the world, making it a better place for all.

Through dedication to these principles, you can experience a life of richness and harmony, characterized by deep connections, fulfilling achievements, and a lasting legacy of positive impact. So embrace this journey with openness, courage, and enthusiasm, ready to transform every moment into an opportunity for growth and joy.

CHAPTER V: Practical Applications

Mindfulness Meditation Practices

Guided Meditations for Radical Acceptance

Mindfulness meditation is a powerful tool for fostering radical acceptance, as it teaches us to observe our thoughts and feelings without judgment or resistance. Guided meditations, in particular, can be especially helpful for beginners or those struggling to maintain focus during meditation. These sessions often involve a narrator guiding the listener through various mental images and scenarios that encourage a deep state of relaxation and acceptance.

One effective guided meditation for radical acceptance involves visualizing a serene landscape, such as a quiet forest or a calm beach. As you mentally walk through this landscape, you are encouraged to notice any discomfort or negative emotions that arise, acknowledging them without trying to change or resist them. This practice helps to reinforce the concept of acceptance as being akin to observing clouds passing in the sky—noticeable, yet transient and not an integral part of the vastness of the sky.

Creating a Meditation Routine

Establishing a consistent meditation routine is key to reaping the benefits of mindfulness. To create a routine, it is important to choose a specific time and place each day for meditation, making it a regular part of your daily schedule. Many find that meditating early in the morning or just before bed helps in making it a routine, as these times generally coincide with quieter moments of the day.

The length of your meditation sessions can vary based on your schedule and comfort level, but starting with just five to ten minutes a day can be effective. As you become more accustomed to the practice, you can gradually increase the duration. It's also helpful to create a comfortable space dedicated to meditation, equipped with a cushion or chair, and perhaps some calming elements such as candles or soft music.

Daily Practices for Self-Compassion

Integrating Acceptance into Daily Life

Integrating acceptance into daily life involves more than just responding passively to events; it requires active engagement with our thoughts and feelings as they arise. This can be practiced through the simple yet profound act of self-awareness. For example, when you notice feelings of impatience or frustration, you can take a moment to acknowledge these feelings, understand their source, and respond to them with kindness rather than criticism.

Another practical way to integrate acceptance is to challenge perfectionist thoughts. When you catch yourself criticizing a perceived flaw or mistake, remind yourself that imperfection is a natural part of being human. Instead of striving for perfection, aim for progress and learning, which are more realistic and forgiving goals.

Exercises for Ongoing Practice

Exercises that can help reinforce daily self-compassion include keeping a gratitude journal, where you regularly record things you appreciate about yourself and your life. Another exercise is the "self-compassion pause," where you take a few moments during stressful situations to speak kindly to yourself, just as you would to a friend in distress. These practices not only enhance self-compassion but also contribute to a more balanced emotional state.

Overcoming Obstacles

Common Challenges and How to Address Them

On the path to radical acceptance, you are likely to encounter several obstacles, such as entrenched habits of self-judgment, emotional resistance, and external pressures. These challenges are normal, but they require conscious strategies to overcome.

One effective approach is to identify specific triggers and patterns of resistance. Once these are recognized, you can develop tailored strategies to address them, such as using mindfulness to remain present during difficult times or seeking support from friends, family, or professionals who can provide perspective and guidance.

Staying Committed to the Path

Staying committed to the practice of radical acceptance and self-compassion, especially when facing obstacles, is crucial. Commitment can be strengthened by setting clear, manageable goals and regularly reflecting on the benefits you have experienced from your practice. Additionally, joining a community or group that practices mindfulness and supports personal growth can provide encouragement and motivation.

It's also important to treat each setback as an opportunity to learn and grow. By reframing challenges as part of the journey rather than signs of failure, you can maintain your commitment and continue to progress towards greater self-acceptance and peace.

Each of these sections provides practical steps and strategies for integrating radical acceptance and self-compassion into everyday life, enabling a journey towards a more fulfilled and peaceful existence. By adopting these practices, you empower yourself to live with greater authenticity and resilience, ready to face life's challenges with grace and composure.

Goodbyes.........

As we reach the conclusion of our exploration into radical acceptance, it is essential to recognize that this is not an endpoint but rather a stepping stone on a continuous journey. The concepts and practices we have discussed are tools to be carried forward, woven into the fabric of everyday life. Radical acceptance is a lifelong commitment to embracing reality as it is, with all its inherent imperfections, challenges, and beauty.

The essence of radical acceptance lies in the profound shift from resisting what is to embracing it fully. This practice is not about passive resignation or giving up on striving for betterment; rather, it is about engaging with life from a place of openness and compassion. By accepting our thoughts, emotions, and experiences without judgment, we create space for healing and transformation. This acceptance allows us to respond to life's inevitable ups and downs with greater equanimity and resilience.

The journey of radical acceptance begins with mindfulness, the practice of being fully present in each moment. Mindfulness teaches us to observe our inner experiences—our thoughts, feelings, and bodily sensations—without trying to change or judge them. This awareness forms the foundation of radical acceptance, enabling us to see our inner world with clarity and compassion. Regular meditation, mindful breathing, and other mindfulness practices help us stay grounded and connected to the present, allowing us to navigate life's challenges with greater ease.

As we integrate mindfulness and radical acceptance into our lives, we encounter numerous opportunities to practice these principles. Each moment, whether joyful or challenging, becomes a chance to embrace reality as it is. This ongoing practice requires patience and dedication, as old habits of resistance and judgment may resurface. When they do, it is important to meet these moments with the same acceptance and compassion we strive to apply to other aspects of our lives. By doing so, we reinforce our commitment to living with greater presence and authenticity.

The journey of radical acceptance also extends to our relationships with others. By accepting people as they are, without trying to change them or impose our expectations, we create more harmonious and fulfilling connections. This acceptance fosters a sense of mutual respect and understanding, allowing for deeper intimacy and trust. It also involves setting healthy boundaries and communicating with compassion, which are essential for maintaining balanced and supportive relationships.

Forgiveness is a significant aspect of radical acceptance, both towards others and ourselves. Forgiving others involves letting go of resentment and anger, freeing us from the emotional burden of past grievances. This process does not mean condoning harmful behavior, but rather acknowledging the hurt and choosing to release it. Similarly, self-forgiveness is crucial for healing and growth. It requires recognizing our mistakes and imperfections, understanding the context of our actions, and allowing ourselves to move forward with a lighter heart.

Living with purpose is another vital element of the ongoing journey of radical acceptance. Discovering what gives our lives meaning and aligning our actions with our core values brings a profound sense of fulfillment and direction. This alignment involves introspection and honesty about what truly matters to us. When we live in accordance with our purpose, we create a life that is not only more meaningful but also more resilient to the inevitable challenges we face.

Cultivating joy and gratitude is equally important on this journey. Joy arises from appreciating the small moments of beauty and connection in daily life, while gratitude shifts our focus from what is lacking to what is abundant. Practices such as keeping a gratitude journal, expressing thanks to others, and consciously acknowledging the positives in our lives enhance our overall sense of well-being and contentment.

The path of radical acceptance is ongoing and ever-evolving. It invites continuous learning and growth, a commitment to facing each moment with openness and equanimity. As you move forward, remember that each step, no matter how small, is progress. Be gentle with yourself as you learn and grow, and be open to the myriad ways in which this journey can enrich your life.

In conclusion, the journey of radical acceptance is one of the most rewarding paths you can undertake. It offers the possibility of a life lived with greater peace, deeper connections, and a more profound sense of purpose. As you continue on this path, may you find the strength to face each moment with acceptance, the courage to embrace your vulnerabilities, and the wisdom to know that you are enough, just as you are.

This journey is yours to shape and define, and it will unfold uniquely for each person. Embrace it with an open heart and a curious mind, allowing the principles of radical acceptance to guide you toward a life of greater harmony and fulfillment. May you find joy in the process, and may the practice of radical acceptance become a source of enduring strength and peace in your life.

As you take these teachings forward, remember that radical acceptance is not about achieving a state of perfection but about embracing the full spectrum of human experience with compassion and grace. It is about living fully in each moment, with all its beauty and all its pain, and knowing that through acceptance, you can find a deeper sense of peace and fulfillment. This is the ongoing journey of radical acceptance—one that offers endless opportunities for growth, healing, and transformation.

With each step you take on this path, you are contributing to a world that values empathy, understanding, and genuine human connection. By practicing radical acceptance, you become a beacon of compassion and wisdom, inspiring others to embark on their own journeys of acceptance and growth. Together, we can create a more compassionate and connected world, one moment of acceptance at a time. So, let us move forward with hope and determination, committed to the ongoing journey of radical acceptance, and open to the boundless possibilities it holds.

Glossary of Terms

Acceptance: The act of acknowledging and embracing reality as it is, without attempting to change, resist, or deny it. Acceptance involves recognizing the present moment and all its complexities, fostering a sense of peace and clarity.

Authenticity: The quality of being genuine, real, and true to oneself. Authenticity involves living in alignment with one's values, beliefs, and true nature, without succumbing to external pressures or societal expectations.

Boundaries: Personal limits that define acceptable behavior and protect one's emotional, physical, and mental well-being. Setting boundaries involves communicating one's needs and limits clearly and respectfully to others.

Compassion: A deep awareness of and desire to alleviate the suffering of others. Compassion involves empathy, kindness, and a willingness to help, both towards oneself and others.

Equanimity: A state of mental calmness, balance, and evenness of temper, especially in difficult situations. Equanimity allows one to maintain composure and clarity amidst chaos and uncertainty.

Forgiveness: The process of letting go of resentment, anger, and the desire for retribution towards oneself or others. Forgiveness involves recognizing and releasing the emotional burdens associated with past hurts, promoting healing and peace.

Gratitude: A feeling of thankfulness and appreciation for the positive aspects of life. Gratitude involves recognizing and acknowledging the good in one's life, which can enhance overall well-being and happiness.

Inner Peace: A state of mental and emotional tranquility, free from the turmoil of stress and anxiety. Inner peace is achieved through practices such as mindfulness, meditation, and self-compassion.

Mindfulness: The practice of being fully present and engaged in the current moment, with an attitude of openness and non-judgment. Mindfulness involves observing one's thoughts, feelings, and surroundings without becoming overwhelmed by them.

Radical Acceptance: A comprehensive and unconditional acceptance of reality, including one's thoughts, feelings, and circumstances. Radical acceptance involves embracing life as it is, without resistance or denial, fostering inner peace and resilience.

Resilience: The capacity to recover quickly from difficulties and adapt to challenging situations. Resilience involves maintaining a positive outlook and using coping strategies to navigate adversity.

Self-Compassion: The practice of being kind and understanding towards oneself, especially during times of failure or difficulty. Self-compassion involves treating oneself with the same care and consideration that one would offer to a friend.

Self-Forgiveness: The process of releasing self-blame and guilt for past mistakes or wrongdoings. Self-forgiveness involves recognizing one's imperfections, learning from the experience, and moving forward with self-compassion.

Self-Judgment: The act of harshly criticizing oneself, often leading to feelings of inadequacy and low self-worth. Overcoming self-judgment involves developing a more compassionate and accepting relationship with oneself.

Self-Worth: The sense of one's own value and worthiness. Self-worth is grounded in the belief that one is inherently valuable and deserving of love and respect, independent of external achievements or validation.

Vulnerability: The willingness to expose oneself to emotional risk, uncertainty, and potential criticism. Embracing vulnerability involves being open and authentic, which can lead to deeper connections and personal growth.

Well-Being: A state of overall health, happiness, and prosperity. Well-being encompasses physical, mental, and emotional health, and is influenced by various factors, including lifestyle choices, relationships, and personal fulfillment.

Wisdom: The ability to make sound decisions and judgments based on knowledge, experience, and understanding. Wisdom involves the application of insight and discernment to navigate life's complexities.

Presence: The state of being fully engaged and attentive in the current moment. Presence involves immersing oneself in the here and now, fostering a deeper connection with one's experiences and surroundings.

Self-Reflection: The process of introspection and examining one's thoughts, feelings, and behaviors. Self-reflection involves gaining insight into oneself, which can lead to personal growth and greater self-awareness.

Empathy: The ability to understand and share the feelings of another. Empathy involves putting oneself in another's shoes and responding with compassion and understanding.

Personal Growth: The ongoing process of developing one's abilities, character, and understanding. Personal growth involves pursuing continuous improvement and self-discovery throughout one's life.

This glossary of terms provides a foundation for understanding the key concepts and practices discussed in the book. As you continue your journey of radical acceptance, refer back to these definitions to reinforce your understanding and application of these essential principles. Each term represents a building block in the construction of a more peaceful, fulfilling, and authentic life.

www.ingramcontent.com/pod-product-compliance
Lightning Source LLC
Chambersburg PA
CBHW051651250726

48653CB00007B/2611